FROM PAT

TO

CHRISTMAS. 1979

THE BATSFORD COLOUR BOOK OF

Ireland

Introduction and commentaries by
Kenneth McNally

B. T. BATSFORD LTD LONDON

First published 1975

© Introduction & commentaries Kenneth McNally 1975

Filmset by Servis Filmsetting Ltd, Manchester
Printed & bound in Great Britain by William Clowes & Sons Ltd, Beccles, Suffolk
for the publishers B. T. Batsford Ltd, 4 Fitzhardinge Street, London W1H 0AH

ISBN 0 7134 2904 6

Contents

Acknowledgments

The Author and Publisher would like to thank the following for their permission to reproduce photographs:
Peter Baker (pp. 45, 47, 49)
Noel Habgood (pp. 27, 37, 53)
Irish Tourist Board (p. 27)
A. F. Kersting (pp. 17, 21, 31)
Northern Ireland Tourist Board (p. 63)
Picturepoint (pp. 21, 35, 39, 43, 45, 59, 61)
Kenneth Scowen (pp. 19, 25, 41)
pages 33, 55 and 57 are from the Author's collection.

Introduction

It is only natural that the visitor to Ireland, whether arriving as a stranger (which he assuredly will not remain for long) or returning as an old and familiar friend, should expect the courtesy of being allowed to form his own opinions of the land and the people. With this in mind let us therefore reject the 'hard sell' approach and declare our hand at the outset. Our brief is straightforward enough: to introduce our country in a sequence of words and pictures, concisely, and at the same time comprehensively – for it has many contrasting facets despite its inherent intimacy – and present it as one would a well-balanced and visually pleasing menu, trusting that the choice will be a representative and fair one. That we put the emphasis on good looks is no accident; for we firmly believe in the old adage that a single picture is worth a thousand words and have confidence in the camera as an able and unbiased reporter. Such, in short, are our terms of reference.

Perhaps we might also mention at this juncture that the word 'tourist' has no place in our preamble. Tourism is, it must be said, a respectable and necessary industry and an important contributor to the economy; but tourists, classed *en masse*, have a way of ending up as anonymous statistics in an official report at the end of the year. No: we expect and require more of our visitors than that, and feel a little flattered that they should choose to spend their leisure time in our company. Irish people tend to regard themselves as personally responsible for the well-being of visitors, rather like unpaid representatives of Bord Failte Eireann (the 'Irish Welcome Board'), and consequently have your best interests at heart. We think nothing of setting aside our own chores – and glad of the opportunity to do so – to discourse on whatever topic takes your fancy, or to advise you on the best place to spend the night, or where to cast your line for the biggest trout. But if you choose to be left alone with your thoughts and lose your identity for a week or two we will not debate your decision, for we are also great respecters of privacy.

When you arrive in Ireland it is more than likely that your first contact with us will be made at a travel terminal of one kind or another, though you may have managed to catch a surreptitious glimpse of our country from the window of your aircraft or the deck of your ship. Travel terminals are notoriously tiresome places at the best of times and hardly conducive to promoting favourable first impressions, but even here you will find that officials are anxious to speed you on your way with the minimum of formalities – the only ones you are likely to encounter during your stay with us.

You will also find, when you set out to discover this island by car, that you can take the road on your own terms, free from traffic congestion and all those other frustrations which contrive to make motoring an onerous pursuit elsewhere. We do have tolerably good roads for the most part and the existing network is constantly being improved, but do not expect to meet perfect surface conditions in every out of the way district you touch. Increasing attention is given to extending scenic routes and many spectacular coastal and mountain drives hitherto inaccessible to motor traffic are now open to exploration. Should you be depending on public transport to get about, then you will be equally well served, for although the system frequently bears the brunt of our own rebukes, things have in reality come a long way since the time of Percy French and his delectable satire on the infamous West Clare Railway. Fast, well-appointed trains speed the modern traveller in comfort to his destination and provide a convenient and relaxing means of viewing the countryside at the same time. Rural bus services, too, are acquiring a new image of efficiency, but not so much so that the driver will insist you get off at the officially designated stop if he can just as readily set you down precisely where you want to go.

The landscape of Ireland is one of great diversity contained in a relatively compact area (for the record, an island measuring only three hundred miles from north to south – if one cheats a little and measures along the diagonal – and under two hundred between its widest east-to-west points: about 32,600 square miles in all). We are scarcely more than a region in some respects, yet we can lay claim to a number of regions and sub-regions within each of the four provinces. This is one of the enduring pleasures of travelling through Ireland, for the passing scene never becomes monotonous or vulgar. Even so, our insular status is inescapable, the characterful coastline is seldom far from sight and at no time more than an hour or two away by car.

How often we look at our landscape and observe only 'scenery', forgetting all the while that man himself, more than any other single factor, has been responsible for shaping it to his precise needs through the ages. And he has accomplished this in a comparatively short span of time. We may not yet fully understand the life style of the primitive food-gatherers of the Middle Stone Age who reached our shores some eight thousand years ago and established themselves along the north-east coast; or of their successor, Neolithic man, who introduced crop production and dabbled in animal husbandry around 3000 BC, but we can be certain that their settlement exercised a positive influence on the shaping of the landscape towards fulfilling our own requirements as an agricultural island first and foremost. This man-made landscape bears the superimposed imprint of different ages and cultures, the characteristics of the one being absorbed or discarded as new systems took over, leaving the debris of the old ways in their wake. Thus the claim of Stone Age man is still with us after 5000 years, evidenced by the great megalithic cairns – the so-called 'giants graves' of north-west Ireland. Later ages, Bronze and Iron, with their transitional phases, are also to be detected in our landscape (though often only by the trained eye) as well as in articles of utilitarian and ornamental use, examples of which have been placed in the permanent safekeeping of museums and art galleries.

The numerous promontory forts around our coasts indicate man's developing possessive attitude and the need to defend his kinfolk from attack. The sites of these structures are often self-evident; in other instances their former location can be pinpointed from the abundance of *dun, doon,* and *doonty* prefixes of Ordnance Survey Map names long after all trace of human occupation has been dispersed. Two of the finest cliff-fort complexes in Ireland are Dun Aonghus on Inishmore (Aran Islands, county Galway) and Dun Kilmore on Achillbeg (county Mayo).

The Early Iron Age saw the emergence of a purely Celtic art form of highly original abstract design, and the arrival of monasticism in the fifth century provided a climate conducive to the furtherance of fine crafts. To the ancient skills it added a totally new dimension – the illuminated manuscript, exemplified by the Book of Kells and other rare survivals. The long monastic era also gave us the remarkable architecture of the Round Towers; these, together with the onetime splendid castles imposed on our landscape by the Norman conquerers, and the strongholds built by the Irish themselves in defiance of the invader, catalogue in mellowed stone the course of an eventful and robust past.

Take away the works of man and we would be left with a scene vastly different to the one we know today. This is not to suggest that all of man's activities have been an enhancement of the land he inherited from nature; one might point to the loss of our once vast forests to make room for agricultural expansion, to say nothing of the much later consequences of urban industrialisation (even if Ireland bears comparatively few scars from this cause). But offset against the debits are the flamboyant splashes of colour man has infused when he introduced new species of flora into the environment. Such compensations must vindicate to some extent man's often devastating onslaught on the landscape as he toiled to make it his own.

If cities were judged on their physical setting, then Dublin with its broad bay and backdrop of mountains must be numbered among Europe's most attractive capitals. It is, appropriately, a thoroughly cosmopolitan city, a status it carries lightly enough without losing sight of its own identity. It is a busy place, but it manages to keep its business dealings discreetly out of sight, knowing full well that it is cast in the role of a well-bred and considerate host. Good breeding and long experience in gracious living are its intrinsic hallmarks. Certainly the Dublin that responded so wholeheartedly to the first performance of *The Messiah* in 1742 was already a highly sophisticated society, discerning in its tastes for the fine arts and acknowledged as a great centre of musical affairs. Handel was aware of this reputation when he presided over the *première* of his famous oratorio here, as were many of his contemporaries, among them the composer Thomas Arne and the celebrated violinist Francesco Geminiani, both of whom lived for several years in the city.

So much for Dublin in the eighteenth century, though one is constantly reminded of that elegant age by the wealth of fine Georgian architecture that dominates many of its spacious squares. Meanwhile, you will no doubt have heard of the convivial atmosphere of Dublin pubs where you can find yourself in earnest conversation with the man sitting next to you before you've sipped the creamy head off your first pint of Guinness. If time permits you might stop off for a drink at McDaid's in Harry Street where playwright and voluble raconteur

Brendan Behan was accustomed to holding court, or drop into Neary's in Chatham Street for oysters with brown bread and butter or a plate of Dublin Bay prawns. But it would be a prejudiced view that represented Dublin as being all pubs and pub talk; and perhaps by way of pre-empting such charges, or maybe in deference to the memory of that redoubtable nineteenth-century temperance campaigner Father Theobald Matthew, whose statue watches over the comings and goings of broad O'Connell Street, the city is blessed with a 'holy hour' each day when licensed premises firmly close their doors to all custom.

If your interest lies in *objets d'art* you will find the hours slipping away unnoticed as you browse among the antique shops off fashionable Grafton Street. And you may well turn up a bargain, for the antique trade in Ireland is still young enough to hold a few surprises in store. For all that Dublin is a city of enlightened outlook and more than a hint of *savoir faire*, you will sense that it is also a place much concerned with its past: its numerous and sometimes remarkable statues are a typical case in point, as is the survival of sizable enclaves of splendid eighteenth-century architecture, though here as elsewhere the threat from development is great, and a matter for constant vigilance on the part of preservationists.

Belfast, the northern capital, lacks the experience of years that gave Dublin its cultural finesse early on and makes no pretentious claims. Being first and foremost a city preoccupied with commerce, Belfast was committed to development along entirely different lines. A healthy economy founded on linen was boosted by the introduction of cotton-spinning in 1777 and this saw the beginnings of a great industrial era. Its merchants were stoic, hard-headed men with their sights resolutely set on economic growth and with little time for frivolity: 'The men have a business look', observed Thackeray in 1842, 'and one sees very few flaunting dandies, as in Dublin.' Belfast, then, has always carried the stamp of a purposeful city; a city of industrialists, sure enough, but also a city of inventors, philanthropists, and visionaries; the Belfast of the Dunlop tyre and the Ferguson tractor, of men who build ships and aircraft, of public benefactors and leaders of men.

From an architectural point of view, Belfast cannot lay claim to a distinguished pedigree. Such highlights as do exist today tend to be the individual survivals – buildings like the Custom House, Queen's University, and even the sometimes maligned City Hall, as well as a handful of others – set precariously in the midst of development proceeding at an urgent pace. Of late, the recently formed Ulster Architectural Heritage Society has maintained a watching brief over this progress to some constraining effect; much, however, has already been irreparably forfeited. In the main, street level architecture tends to be dull, principally because lower storeys fall victim to modernisation in shopping thoroughfares. But look higher up on the facades of Belfast's buildings and discover an entirely different world of rich and exuberant ornament. Architectural sculpture flourished in the Victorian city at the hands of brilliant craftsmen like Thomas Fitzpatrick and Harry Hems, who recognised the importance of creating buildings to be looked at as well as lived in.

Belfast is a convenient and logical starting point from which to explore the Ulster countryside. To the north the lovely sweep of the Antrim coast road strings together a series of picturesque villages and secluded summer resorts and gives access to the breathtaking Nine Glens (a sure way of starting a debate in a pub in these parts is to ask a group of local men to put names to the nine). Over in the west of the Province the Fermanagh Lakeland is only now coming into its own as a vast natural recreation area; and from here the grandeur of the Donegal Highlands is within easy reach. Nor must we omit from our passing survey the Mourne Mountains of county Down, apple blossom time in county Armagh and the elegant city itself with its two cathedrals, and the perennially popular holiday centres of Portrush and Bangor.

Irish is the first official language of the twenty-six county Republic, but English, recognised as the second official and 'alternative' language, is in fact the most widely used in everyday life. The study of Irish is compulsory in State schools, and a standard of competence in the subject is required in certain professions; but despite this emphasis, and although one will *see* plenty of evidence of the national language (as, for example, on public signs, place names, etc., where both Irish and English words manage to coexist) it would be a remote part of the country indeed where a stranger could not make himself understood.

The Irish language, therefore, holds a tenuous position in the affairs of modern Ireland, and while present-day influences tend to be blamed for its decline, and the decline of Gaelic culture generally, in reality the cause is deeply rooted in history. The golden age of the

Bardic poets who so enriched our literature in mediaeval times gave way under the pressures of the penal laws to the more ephemeral utterances of peasant poets and ballad singers. This departure from the formal literary tradition was earthy and of the people, and while it lacked the discipline of the élite Bardic scholars it nevertheless became for a time an effective bulwark against the complete erosion of Gaelic culture in the country.

The real threat to the language came in the nineteenth century. The 1800 Act of Union brought Ireland finally and firmly under the control of a British parliament. Country people began increasingly to speak English in their dealings with landlords and incoming settlers; and when the National Board of Education was established in 1831 to extend state supervised education throughout the land, Irish was conspicuously absent from the curriculum of its schools. The disastrous famine of the 1840s dealt a further demoralising blow to the language by fragmenting family and kinship ties through death and emigration. To be unable to speak English came to be looked on as a social stigma and as the century progressed great masses of the population turned away from their heritage. Not long before, the fashionable lyric poet Tom Moore had ably exploited the mood of nostalgia felt for the suppressed Gaelic tradition in verses full of a plaintive hankering after days and glories gone for ever. Moore's *Melodies* appealed to a society content to be dazzled by the enchantèd 'light of other days', but he himself failed to penetrate the essence of the Gaelic legacy, his charming verses owe little to the ancient poetry of Ireland and had slight relevance alongside the pioneering work of later poets like Mangan, Davis and Ferguson, who laid the foundations of a great revival in Irish literature. In 1893 the Gaelic League was formed by Douglas Hyde to promote interest in the Irish language, the arts and sport, and there followed an exciting and vital period for literature with the emergence of such eminent writers as Synge, Yeats, O'Casey, Joyce, and others who were to draw extensively on the rich store of ancient Irish texts then only coming to light through copious translations by a new generation of Gaelic scholars. Yeats in particular seized on this material for inspiration and fused it with his own writing to produce a new and essentially Irish idiom.

But while the Gaelic League was instrumental in breathing new life into a flagging culture, it was less successful in its wider aims of restoring the Irish language to the ordinary people. That objective became the concern of the Gaeltacht Commission, a state-controlled body set up in 1925 to encourage spoken Irish, especially along the western seaboard where remoteness of situation had insulated many Gaelic-speaking communities against outside influences. Selected areas were designated *Gaeltachts* and qualify for attractive incentive grants for housing, education, home-based industry, and other social benefits. Today, however, the *Gaeltachts* are dwindling in extent as rural populations are thinned by a movement to more centralised townships, and, of course, by emigration. The total abandonment of many small islands off the west coast in recent years has been a crucial factor in this trend. Nevertheless, it is still possible to hear a very pure Irish spoken in parts of Donegal, Mayo, and (particularly) the Aran Islands, as well as in some southerly counties, such as Cork and Kerry.

West of the Shannon lies an entirely different Ireland: different from the eastern half of the country in so many ways, a stark contrast to the exceptionally rich farmlands of Meath, the tree-clad valleys of Wicklow, the industrialised north, and different, not least, in the outlook of its people; for the west of Ireland is the last outpost of Europe both in terms of geography and social environment. Strictly speaking, 'the west' must take into account such scenic spectaculars as the formidable Cliffs of Moher and the desolate Burren country of county Clare, while parts of Donegal might equally make a strong claim on our purview. Be that as it may, the essence of the west of Ireland is found within the ragged boundaries of Connacht, and for the many who have discovered it no other place bears comparison.

Connacht is a wild, expansive province with a particularly unkempt look about it, though it has by contrast several sophisticated townships gathered about its seaward margins. One might select for mention Galway and Westport as examples of thriving, forward-looking communities with a lively history of trading and social intercourse. But the interior of this region is dominated by mountain and bog and a scattering of lakes, altogether uncompromising terrain which daunted even the Norman invaders at the outset and which in later centuries was apportioned among transplanted dissidents to mould into shape as best they could. As a province it has a long history of neglect, its inherently poor soils have for the most part made the task of wresting a livelihood from the land an arduous and unrewarding one, and it is not surprising that emigration has traditionally been heaviest from this part of Ireland. A perceptive nineteenth-century traveller noted that everything in Connacht is on a grand scale – 'except the works of man'. Yet even in the most unlikely locations man has made good his claim to the land and survives from generation to generation.

One speaks thus of Connacht in general terms, but it is well to remember that within its boundaries are sub-regions of great diversity. Connemara perhaps comes most readily to mind as by far the best introduction to Connacht, with its limewashed gables and golden thatch, the pattern of drystone walls tightly hemming tiny fields, and a vivid flora; a totally compelling landscape never without interest. But then Connemara is so well known, if only by name and hearsay, that to dwell on its many faces would be to reiterate what has been said and written time and time again. In any case Connemara needs little introduction; it can and does speak for itself.

Mayo, the most north-westerly county of this province, and indeed in Ireland – for its massive right-angled buttress projects far into the Atlantic – is less familiar territory, but it never fails to captivate visitors who stray this far north from Galway. The county town is Castlebar, a busy, prosperous place with all the air of a rural capital, and an annual song contest that is one of the major festivals of the year in these parts. The road northwards from Castlebar leads through Mallaranny to the Corraun Peninsula and Achill Island. A causeway and road-bridge connect Achill to the mainland, but in all other respects it preserves its insular identity. Achill is the largest Irish island, some fifty-seven square miles of ancient Pre-Cambrian hills and peat-filled valleys, dotted with brackish lakes and rock outcrop, and bounded by precipitous cliffs and broad beaches of smooth clean sand. It is an island of superlatives, a holiday island *par excellence*, and each year welcomes many thousands of visitors with memorable hospitality.

You may notice, as you travel through the west, vacant cottages with boarded-up windows and padlocked doors: these are the emigrant's binding link with his birthright, the visual evidence of the Irishman's traditional attachment to his land; and he does not sell out in case one day he wishes to come home. Emigration has long been an indelible aspect of life in western Ireland, and for almost as long has had its share of critics who regard it as a national evil, though it was welcomed warmly enough in the nineteenth century when the only alternative was starvation. Nowadays such destitution is unknown and the resort to emigration carries less chilling overtones, the way having been paved by generations of kinfolk who have won for themselves and their families the right to self respect in their adopted land. Many do, indeed, make the return journey after maybe ten or twenty or more years in Boston, or Cleveland, or Philadelphia, or any one of a dozen other places where Irish communities have established little colonies overseas.

Connacht is fine peat country yielding rich dark turves under the cutter's spade, or 'slane', and which, when fanned by the Atlantic breezes and warmed by the sun, dry as hard compact blocks of fuel for winter fires. Cutting takes place in spring when great tracts of bog-land become a scene of intense human activity and drying turf stacks contribute a distinctive element to the landscape. Bog cotton, purple moor grass, and deer's hair grass are typical colonisers, providing a measure of relief against the sombre monotones of cut-over peat land.

Peat, or as it is more generally called in Ireland, turf, has for centuries been the traditional fuel of country people and it is customary for families living in rural areas to hold turbary rights to sections of bog from which they 'win' their supplies of turf for use in the home. In many instances these concessions are of long-standing origin, having been inherited through successive generations; and such is their continuing social significance in the economy of small isolated communities, especially in the west, that these interests are safeguarded by the Irish Land Commission. Considerable though the scale of domestic usage is, it is now secondary to the commercial exploitation of peat bogs by Bord na Mona, a government controlled body which supplies harvested and processed peat in various forms to meet the demand from power-generating stations, industry, and the urban domestic market (you will see bales of peat briquettes in most consumer stores in the Republic), while the marketing of peat moss as a soil additive is an important horticultural outlet. In a country having negligible coal resources peat is naturally a most valuable alternative (even though its calorific value is rather less than half that of coal); but it is not an unlimited one. Even if consumer demand remained at its present level it is estimated that denudation of the vast central bogs will be complete by the end of the century or shortly after. Less accessible tracts, like the rolling blanket bogs of the west, are capable of supplying the domestic needs of farming communities for much longer, being unsuited to large-scale commercial exploitation.

It was the climatic conditions of post-glacial times which favoured peat accumulation in the first place, and climate continues to exercise a powerful influence on our landscape to give it that distinctive freshness – one might even say 'Irishness' – so much admired by visitors. The climate of Ireland is the most equable in Europe, experiencing no great extremes from one end of the year to the other. A moist, clean atmosphere, characteristic of our oceanic situation, is encouraged by the warming influence of the North Atlantic Drift and finds visual outlet in the greenery of healthy grassland and foliage, and reveals itself further in the colourful and exotic flora of the south-west. This bonus is ample compensation for the frequent (though seldom excessive) rainfall. Mild winters are another benefit conferred by our maritime circumstance; frost and snow are rare visitors to the western seaboard and perhaps not surprisingly many of its off-shore islands are the winter refuge of several species of migratory birds. Statistics show that on the whole we receive slightly less uninterrupted sunshine than many parts of Britain, and broken cloud cover is common throughout the year. But the pattern of our skies is rarely stationary: wind is a prominent feature of the Irish climate and is constantly at work keeping clouds on the move to allow the sun to break through, sometimes at the most unexpected moments.

Our preliminaries are concluded. Enthusiasm, hopefully, has been kept in check, for it is not our intention to hold out false promises but to state our case plainly in the manner we know best. Much of course remains unsaid, and much that has been said barely scratches the surface. But as we have already pointed out, our purpose is one of introduction; the acquaintance on which lasting friendships are settled cannot be made at second hand. On the pages that follow you will find inspiration for a vicarious journey through the provinces and counties, stopping off at cities and villages, seaports and islands, ancient monuments, and frequently pausing to take in the breadth of open landscapes, clear to the horizon. The pictures do more than lend weight to our claims, they tell their own story, convincingly and uniquely, and whet the appetite in anticipation of a journey to be made.

O'CONNELL BRIDGE, DUBLIN

The River Liffey flows in a westerly direction after leaving its source in the Wicklow Hills, then abruptly changes its mind and doubles back towards the east, following a course that takes it through the centre of Dublin to pass beneath a dozen or so bridges before being swallowed up in Dublin Bay.

O'Connell Bridge is the principal artery linking the north and south sides of the city. The first great bridge was built here in 1791 by James Gandon and was called Carlisle Bridge; in 1880 some of the original features, including the decorative keystones by Edward Smyth, were discarded when the bridge was enlarged to accommodate the increase in traffic. The name was also changed at that time. Its rebuilt width is now greater than its 150 foot span, and the little raised concrete islands in the middle have become a welcome and very necessary haven for pedestrians. The width of the bridge now matches that of O'Connell Street itself, which, Dubliners will tell you, is the widest city thorough-fare in Europe; and with so much traffic to cope with at rush hour when it undoubtedly becomes the busiest place in all Ireland, the claim may well have an element of truth.

At the north approach to the bridge, and framed in our picture by two contrasting street lamps, stands the great bronze statue of Daniel O'Connell (the 'Liberator'), sculptured by John Henry Foley. The symbolic group of figures gathered about the pedestal are the work of Thomas Brock.

THE CUSTOM HOUSE, DUBLIN

Built between 1781 and 1791 by James Gandon, the imposing Custom House epitomizes the great era of prosperity and elegance that Dublin knew in the latter half of the eighteenth century. It is by any reckoning an outstanding building, and one of which any capital city could be justly proud. Even before it was completed, the *Dublin Evening Post* heralded it as 'the first edifice of its kind in Europe'. The Custom House is exceptionally rich in ornament; of particular interest are the keystone decorations comprising a series of carved heads representing the Atlantic Ocean and 13 Irish rivers. They are the work of Edward Smyth, whose splendid architectural sculpture was henceforth to grace numerous other public buildings designed by Gandon in Dublin during that architect's long and distinguished association with the city.

In 1921 the Custom House was the target of an incendiary attack which completely gutted the interior and destroyed volumes of British administrative records. Some time afterwards, the Republic's Office of Public Works restored the building to its former grandeur, but with certain variations in points of detail; the interior in particular was much altered. To the left of the picture on the quayside, and dwarfing the passing traffic, massive Guinness containers await shipment on the *Lady Patricia*.

TRINITY COLLEGE, DUBLIN

The University of Dublin was founded in 1591 by Elizabeth I following representations by Archbishop Ussher. The buildings were erected on the site formerly occupied by the ancient priory of All Hallows and were ready for the first intake of students in 1594. Since that time the College has undergone several major phases of reconstruction, notably in the eighteenth century, and nothing of the original remains.

Taken together, the elements of our picture fitly represent a century and a half of architectural development. We are looking through the high arch of the splendid main entrance façade (built in 1759 to designs by Henry Keene and John Sanderson) to the elegant Campanile erected in 1853 by Lord John Beresford, Primate of Ireland and Chancellor of the University. The Campanile now contains the Great Bell of the College, taken from the old belfry, and reputedly stands on the precise location of the old priory church. Beyond, faintly discernible in the background, are the red-brick buildings known as the Rubrics; built around 1700 (with late nineteenth-century renovation of the top storey), this is the oldest surviving part of Trinity.

The Library of the College is said to rank among the great libraries of the world. The collection was started at the beginning of the seventeenth century when a gift of £700 was presented to the University by the English army to mark the defeat of the Spaniards at Kinsale and the quelling of the Munster rising. Pre-eminent among many priceless treasures in this vast collection is the eighth-century illuminated manuscript of the Book of Kells; this, together with other works of national and historic interest, is on daily display to visitors.

GLENDALOUGH ROUND TOWER, COUNTY WICKLOW

This beautiful glen, called 'the Valley of the Two Lakes', was the secluded retreat selected by Saint Kevin for a hermitage in the sixth century. Before long, however, his renown attracted a large following and Glendalough developed into an important ecclesiastical settlement and a place of pilgrimage. Its remoteness did not save it from the attentions of the Vikings, and several raids are known to have occurred in the ninth and tenth centuries; while torrential floods in 1174 caused considerable damage to the buildings. The two lakes of the valley are linked by the Gleneala River which in turn flows on to unite with the Avonmore River and eventually the famed 'meeting of the waters' in the Vale of Avoca.

The 103 ft Round Tower is in an excellent state of preservation, complete with its (reconstructed) conical roof. Tall mature conifers and lush vegetation flourish in this sheltered location.

TYRRELSPASS, COUNTY WESTMEATH

A quiet, well-kept, late eighteenth-century village of distinctive layout about 12 miles from the county town of Mullingar. Tyrrelspass was the inspiration of the Countess of Belvedere who had the township planned in the form of a crescent and flanking a pleasant tree-shaded green which remains the focal point of the village. The family is remembered in a resplendent monument in the attractive 'Planters Gothic' church; Belvedere House itself is less than ten miles distant at the eastern margin of Lough Ennell and is notable for its fine gardens.

But the name of the village is much older and recalls the Anglo-Norman family of Tyrrel who here maintained a strategic castle (still to be seen to the west of the village) from the fifteenth century. In 1597, Richard Tyrrel and Piers Lacy at the head of an insurgent force surprised and utterly defeated a 1,000-strong English army under Christopher Barnewall at a crucial pass through the nearby peat bogs. The influence of the Tyrrels came to an end in the seventeenth century when most of their land was forfeited in the Cromwellian confiscations.

MUIREADACH'S CROSS, MONASTERBOICE, COUNTY LOUTH

Monasterboice, some six miles from Drogheda, owes its origin as a monastic settlement to Saint Buithe of the fifth century. As is not infrequently the case, its early history is obscure and it only finds its way into our annals from the year 759; but the site is principally distinguished by its outstanding Irish High Crosses. Muireadach's Cross, the one shown here, is the finest of the group and is so called after a tenth-century abbot of that name who, in the words of the translated inscription, 'caused the cross to be made'. It measures 17 feet 8 inches high and is richly decorated with scriptural themes. Among the episodes depicted on this the west face are the Arrest of Christ and the Crucifixion; and panels portraying such biblical personages as Saint Peter, Doubting Thomas, and Moses. It is likely that in their original state the figures were highlighted in vivid colours after the fashion of the beautiful illuminated manuscripts belonging to the monastic era; a thousand years of exposure to the elements has however removed all hint of their former splendour.

Associated ruins close by include those of two minor churches and an imposing Round Tower still more than 100 feet high, even though deprived of its topmost section.

MWEELREA MOUNTAINS FROM NEAR RINVYLE, COUNTY GALWAY

Our prospect embraces two counties: the Mweelrea Mountains flank the south-west boundary of Mayo, the deep gash of Killary inlet providing a convenient dividing line between maritime Galway and Mayo. This great range of hills rises splendidly to 2,688 feet, the loftiest summit in all Connacht, surpassing even mighty Croaghpatrick in height. Extensive views reward the climber; to the south lie the Twelve Bens and Maumturk ranges, sprawling dramatically across much of Connemara, while away to the west and north the scene is one of small islands set delicately in the broad Atlantic – Inishbofin, Inishturk, Caher and Clare; and in clear conditions the long spiny finger of Achill Head can be distinguished in the distance.

Here, in the vicinity of Rinvyle, the essential characteristics of the Connemara landscape are well displayed. The rough stony ground supplies the farmer with all he needs to build his field walls and live-stock enclosures; and, indeed, many of the older cottages still in use have been constructed entirely with materials zealously gleaned from the little plots on which they stand. Rye thatch remains much in evidence, even though modern Land Commission housing (of the type seen at the extreme right-hand margin of our view) resorts to the more enduring, if far less picturesque slate roofs.

BUNRATTY CASTLE, COUNTY CLARE

Situated on the banks of the Owenogarney or Ratty River, some eight miles from the town of Limerick, Bunratty Castle is a magnificent fifteenth-century keep of the O'Briens of Thomond who held this site from 1355. The setting and prospect are most picturesque, and in the seventeenth century the imposing building with its landscaped gardens attracted widespread acclaim.

The external appearance is of a rather formidable fortress of rectangular plan, having corner turrets joined in pairs on the north and south faces. Inside the castle is some very fine stucco work. Recent renovation has been carried out and for several years this great building has echoed to the sounds of twentieth-century minstrels recreating something of the past glories of the castle and its history for the benefit of paying guests at mediaeval banquets. Traditional fare is served up on wooden platters, and diners eat their meal with the aid of a dirk (conventional cutlery is taboo here) while earthenware goblets are frequently replenished with sweet mead by attentive serving wenches. The penalty for unruly behaviour is a spell in the dungeon; but, on the other hand, a show of exemplary manners combined with a dash of *savoir faire* may lead to one being elevated to the status of Earl for the evening (coronet and robe by courtesy of the management).

ACHILL ISLAND, COUNTY MAYO

Achill is the largest of all the Irish islands and the most westerly inhabited landmass in Europe. It is a holiday island of international repute, and each summer attracts thousands of visitors from Britain, the Continent and America, as well as being a favourite resort with Irish people north and south. This Atlantic outpost has the convenience of a causeway and road-bridge connecting it to the mainland, while an internal network of 100 miles of hard-surfaced roads provides access to some of the most spectacular coastal drives in the county. Achill's extreme north-westerly latitude results in slightly longer hours of daylight – a bonus much appreciated by holidaymakers.

This view of the island is typical of the sheltered south-east coast where the calm waters of the Sound provide a safe anchorage for small boats at Cloghmore (the name, appropriately, means 'the big stones'), an area abounding in colourful lichen-encrusted rocks. Seaweed is harvested along this shoreline for sale to the alginate processing factory at nearby Newport and provides an additional source of income for a few of the island's farmers and fishermen. Neat slated cottages hug the water's edge, shielded from the prevailing south-westerly winds by an arpeggio of minor hills, and large turf stacks are conspicuously sited close to the houses, ready to hand for winter fires.

DRUMCLIFF CHURCHYARD, COUNTY SLIGO

Occupying the former site of an ancient monastery attributed to Saint Columcille, about five miles from the town of Sligo, Drumcliff church-yard is today a place of modern pilgrimage as the last resting place of the poet William Butler Yeats. When, in 1939, Yeats died in the south of France, he was buried at Roquebrune; but in accordance with his wishes his remains were brought back to his beloved Sligo countryside and reinterred here in 1948. The grave lies in a tree-shaded spot close to the church 'under bare Ben Bulben's head' (the dramatic flat-topped mountain to the north-east that makes frequent appearance in Irish legend), and the enigmatic epitaph on the simple limestone slab is that prescribed by the poet himself:

> *Cast a cold eye*
> *On life, on death*
> *Horseman, pass by!*

Nearby is a sculptured High Cross dating from the tenth century and depicting Old and New Testament themes; on the west side of the main Sligo-Bundoran road a shorn-off Round Tower is all that remains of the monastery buildings.

BALLYNESS BAY, COUNTY DONEGAL

The lovely undulating countryside between Horn Head and Bloody Foreland in north-west Donegal is well known to visitors from near and far; it seldom fails to impress the newcomer and often draws him back time and time again to this special corner of Ireland. The muted colours of this soft landscape, with its chequered pattern of small-field cultivation interspersed with rock outcrop and heather, is set off to fine effect by narrow margins of sandy shoreline washed clean by the tides. Thatch roofs are still traditional in these parts and much care is lavished on maintaining the neat appearance of homely cottages.

This is ideal climbing country: Errigal (2,466 feet) and Muckish (2,197 feet) offer challenging conditions, as well as unrivalled views of the countryside spread out below and of remote, frequently storm-bound Tory Island some eight miles off the coast to the north. Several comfortable centres of accommodation are nearby – Dunglow, Falcarragh, Dunfanaghy and Carrigart.

CROAGHPATRICK, COUNTY MAYO

This massive and dramatically contoured quartzite mountain takes its name from Ireland's patron saint who reputedly fasted on its summit for 40 days in 441 in the course of his journey through Connacht. Today the mountain is a scene of annual pilgrimage in July (Garland Sunday) when tens of thousands of people of all ages climb the 2,510 feet high peak, sometimes barefoot, making 'stations' at various holy mounds during the ascent, and again at the top where there is a small modern chapel.

Croaghpatrick is set amid some of the loveliest coast-bound scenery of Mayo. It turns a bold north-west face to the sea and overlooks picturesque Clew Bay with its myriad islands (365 in popular hearsay – 'one for every day of the year'), while to the east and south its shoulders relax to give way to less formidable slopes leading down to little patches of cultivation isolated by vast expanses of bogland, relieved here and there with tiny lakes. The maritime climate favours a colourful flora, but tree and shrub growth is severely stunted by prevailing south-westerly winds and seldom achieves mature height.

The principal town of the district is Westport, about six miles distant, a popular sea-angling resort and a convenient centre from which to explore the county Mayo highlands. Westport House, designed by Richard Cassels and built in 1730 (with later modifications by James Wyatt, who laid out the town itself towards the end of the eighteenth century) is one of Connacht's showpieces and may be visited in summer months.

KINSALE HARBOUR, COUNTY CORK

Kinsale, situated on the Bandon Estuary, has all the air of an old aristo-crat who has known rather better days. The essential charm of this quiet resort lies in its acceptance of the fact that it has not moved with the times; for although it can point to a noble pedigree it does not strive at keeping up appearances, even if its one-time penchant for gracious living is still evidenced by some fine Georgian dwelling-houses within the town. The general mood here is one of total relaxation, making Kinsale an ideal centre for an altogether leisurely holiday. It is also noted for its unrivalled deep-sea angling and not surprisingly numbers a high proportion of fishermen among its seasonal visitors. Summer Cove, an aptly named little bay about one mile to the east of the town, is a popular bathing place.

In 1601, Kinsale was taken over by invading Spaniards who, with the help of Hugh O'Neill of Ulster, held out against a relieving English force for three months until finally overwhelmed by Mountjoy. A legacy of Spanish names recalls the incident. And it was at Kinsale that James II landed in 1689 to begin his ill-fated attempt at reinstate-ment, with such disastrous consequences at the river Boyne one year later. When Kinsale ceased to be a strategic British naval base at the end of the eighteenth century it forfeited much of its prestige and lapsed into a state of semi-retirement from the affairs of the outside world.

ROCK OF CASHEL, COUNTY TIPPERARY

This massive outcropping of limestone, theatrically topped by a great church and fort complex, has a particularly Continental look about it and invariably comes as something of a surprise to travellers catching sight of it for the first time. The ancient site was held for seven centuries by the Kings of Cashel and Munster, descendants of Conall Corc who established the original fortification here in the latter half of the fourth century. The Rock has a long history of ecclesiastical associations: Saint Patrick baptized the King of Cashel (probably Aengus, or his predecessor Corc the third) at this place in 450 or thereabouts, and later centuries saw the establishment ruled by kings who were also abbots. In 1101, Muirchertach O'Brien ceded the Rock to the Church and it became the episcopal See of Munster.

The extant buildings comprise Cormac's Great Church, or Chapel (placed at the centre of our viewpoint), built between 1127 and 1134 and regarded as one of the finest examples of Irish Romanesque Architecture; a thirteenth-century Gothic cathedral supplanting an earlier church built by Donal Mor O'Brien in 1169; a Round Tower of tenth-century date; and the ruin of an 80 ft high castle. An unusual High Cross with heavily weathered sculptures stands near the south entrance to the cathedral.

UPPER LAKE, KILLARNEY, COUNTY KERRY

A century and more of travel literature of one kind or another must, it would seem, have said all there is to say about Killarney; yet, in retrospect, it appears to have said very little beyond stating the obvious. Even experienced travellers tend to become a little inhibited when faced with the task of reporting back on their impressions of the place, and all because Killarney is essentially a very individual experience which cannot be conveniently (or at any rate convincingly) reduced to a straightforward equation. Well indeed might the credibility of our earlier analogy that a single picture is worth a thousand words be called into question here, for Killarney has so many facets and fleeting moods that to select but one is surely to be guilty of negligence of a sort.

The timeless attraction of Killarney lies in the infinite variety of its landscape. It is a vast natural recreation area that calls for unhurried exploration; consequently, modern transport is abandoned in favour of jaunting cars, row-boats, and ponies, all-in-all a leisurely progression through miles of wooded hillsides, expansive lakes and tumbling waterfalls. Upper Lake is the smallest of the group of three: some 430 acres in extent it nestles in the heart of lush, exotic vegetation, overlooked by Purple Mountain and the Mangerton range of hills. Here and there are small islets crowded with Arbutus, which flourishes in this its most northern European station. There is colour aplenty at all seasons, and even in all weathers, and when the sun is hidden by cloud and overcast conditions prevail the lakes take on the delicate hues of a watercolour painting, all the more enhanced by the transient shades of evening light.

COBH HARBOUR, COUNTY CORK

Cobh, the sheltered cove of Cork, was so called until 1849 when Queen Victoria visited the ancient port and its name was changed with expedient fervour to Queenstown. In 1922, following hard on the heels of Irish Independence, the original name was reinstated; such was also the case with Kingstown (now Dun Laoghaire once more), but the imperial legacy has not been entirely obliterated, the monarchal names cropping up now and then on durable items of hotel cutlery and the like.

A magnificent natural setting and agreeable climate make Cobh a popular holiday centre, particularly with sailing and boating enthusiasts, while the proximity of Cork City (14 miles) supplies the sophistication of modern shops and entertainments. Perched dramatically above the waterfront is the Cathedral of Saint Colman, a late nineteenth-century Gothic Revival building with some fine internal features and a remarkable 42 bell carillon having a range of two and a half octaves. The Cathedral occupies a strategic vantage point with especially good views across the estuary: from here can be seen the Irish Naval Base of Haulbowline Island (co-ordinating centre for marine rescue and defence) and ominous Spike Island where in the last century scores of hapless convicts embarked for the fearful voyage to Botany Bay and a lifetime of penal servitude. Ironically, it was also from Cobh that a new era of comfortable sea travel was inaugurated in 1838 with the first transatlantic steamship sailing by the *Sirius*.

ROSSBEIGH STRAND, GLENBEIGH, COUNTY KERRY

This glorious curve of sandy beach occupies most of Rossbeigh (Ros Behy, the 'headland of the birches') jutting out into Dingle Bay. It is a superb bathing strand some two miles in extent, washed by white-tipped waves and strung with sandhills having convenient hollows for sunbathing and picnics. The beautiful Kerry mountains are never out of sight and form an impressive backdrop to the scene.

Less than two miles away is the secluded village of Glenbeigh with all the ingredients for a restful holiday, such as golf, sea-fishing, and gentle country walks amid breathtaking countryside. To the south is the exhilarating 'Glenbeigh Horseshoe', a route for the energetic, taking in Drung Hill and Seefin Mountain with its shapely ice-chiselled corries. Also close at hand is Glencar and lovely Lake Caragh, Macgillacuddy's Reeks and Windy Gap, while to the north of this district lies the long arm of the Dingle Peninsula, a wonderful coastal drive affording good views of Dingle Bay and, from its most westerly point, the Blasket Islands.

ARDMORE ROUND TOWER, COUNTY WATERFORD

This is a late example of Round Tower design exhibiting graceful proportions and having certain departures from the norm, such as the protruding horizontal coursing which serves to indicate the levels of the various storeys. The interior is unusual for the sculptured heads on the corbel stones. The 95-feet high Tower commands a most advantageous situation close to the sea with a restful prospect of sandy coves and gently sloping fields round about. The early association with Saint Declan has gained a deal of renown for the site as a place of pilgrimage.

Adjoining the Round Tower, Saint Declan's Church ruins mark the location of an important monastic foundation. The church, or cathedral, has architectural features attributable to the tenth to fourteenth centuries and is particularly notable for the remarkable Romanesque arcading incorporating a group of figure carvings, much weathered, but with clearly depicted themes, on the outside west gable. Other remains include Declan's Holy Well and Stone; and Temple Disert, a hermitage church close to the cliff face. History apart, this is an area very conducive to rest and meditation well away from the pressures of modern life.

THE MOURNE MOUNTAINS, COUNTY DOWN

The Mournes are an accommodating range of mountains: accommodating in that they present themselves as readily accessible for walking and climbing without the frustration of preliminary foothills to be negotiated; accommodating to the compact little townships that find just enough space to coexist around the seaward periphery; and accommodating in the far-reaching vistas opening up from their easily attained summits, particularly on a crisp clear day when a visibility range of up to 100 miles is not unusual. Spreading out from the base of the mountains, here seen from the south-west, the countryside is a colourful patchwork of neat hedge-bordered fields dotted with low-crouching farmsteads and grazing livestock, and hillsides clumped with yellow whin.

In 1896, the genial songwriter Percy French penned a set of verses destined to carry the name of Mourne to distant horizons; but at least half a century earlier the mountains were already making a name for themselves as a rich source of dressed granite, and for a time a thriving export trade in slabs and setts for roadmaking projects was carried on here and the quarries prospered, providing much local employment. And while Percy French's disillusioned young Irish emigrant might lament his failure to find the streets of London paved with gold, he could have been reasonably certain, had he ventured further north, of finding the streets of industrial Lancashire paved with friendly Mourne granite.

QUEEN'S UNIVERSITY, BELFAST

This was one of three 'Queen's Colleges' established in 1845 (the others were Cork and Galway) to meet Nonconformist and Catholic pressures for education at university level. The Belfast building, now an independent University, was completed in 1849 to designs by Sir Charles Lanyon, and though certain features of the original plan were forfeited under a cost-conscious administration, the result nevertheless remains one of the city's architectural highlights.

The red-brick Tudor style building is prominently situated on University Road, one mile from the centre of Belfast. The beautifully proportioned tower with its leaded windows above the main entrance houses the Vice-Chancellor's office and is modelled on the Founder's Tower of Magdalen College, Oxford. In 1868 a Library Hall was added by W. H. Lynn, and since that time and particularly within the last quarter century many new extensions have been built to accommodate the increasing intake of students. A very functional modern Library, just visible above the rooftops to the left of the central tower, is one of the more recent additions to the complex; but for undergraduates and laymen alike, 'Queen's' invariably means the familiar red-brick building around which the life of the University revolves.

CUSHENDUN, COUNTY ANTRIM

As well as being a much-frequented summer resort, Cushendun is also notable as the home of Agnes Skryne, better known as Moira O'Neill, 'the poetess of the glen'. Her nostalgic *Songs of the Glens of Antrim* well evoke the changing moods of the beautiful countryside round about: a landscape of lush hillsides and winding rivers, tree-fringed meadows and snug farmsteads overlooking a broad curving bay. Moira O'Neill lived at Rockport House, the neat slate-roofed building crouching low in the greenery of our picture and situated close to the beach with fine sea views.

Just across the blue waters of the bay is Cushendun village with its gleaming white houses and hotels. In the far distance the distinctive outline of Garron Point is visible, and to complete this idyllic scene a touch of romantic history is supplied by the dark ivy-shrouded ruin of Carra Castle, where tradition has it Sean the Proud O'Neill was slain by his old enemies the MacDonnells in 1567. The entire area is now in the care of the National Trust.

PORTSTEWART, COUNTY DERRY

Originally called in Irish 'the Port of the Green Headland', Portstewart occupies a most advantageous situation to the east of the estuary of the river Bann, and is sheltered from the chilling north winds that frequently blow in from the Atlantic. In the early part of the nineteenth century it was little more than an undistinguished hamlet, but soon after that time Henry O'Hara and John Cromie began to develop the township as a fashionable summer resort. One of O'Hara's more extravagant gestures was to build a large sham fortress overlooking the town and bay to indulge his taste for the romantic; though hardly a beautiful structure, it is not without impressive features, and is at present used as a convent.

In 1842, James Makepeace Thackeray visited Portstewart and found in it 'an air of comfort and neatness which is seldom seen in Ireland'. However, he felt compelled to tilt at the strict, and to his way of thinking, excessive sabbath observances and particularly singled out for criticism the amount of scandalmongering he encountered. It might perhaps be added that Portstewart today retains those qualities which so pleased Thackeray, while it has outgrown much of the inward provincialism he found distasteful. It offers variety in plenty to the holidaymaker: excellent sea-bathing, a wide range of accommodation, facilities for boating, fishing, tennis and golf, and a lively night life. To the east and west of the town are panoramic views of what the novelist Charles Lever called 'the awful sublimity' of this 'iron bound' coast.

THE GIANT'S CAUSEWAY, COUNTY ANTRIM

Less than three miles from the little county Antrim town of Bushmills (of liqueur whiskey fame) and tucked into an accommodating corner of this beautiful coast, is the geological phenomenon known far and near as the Giant's Causeway. The formation, though not unique, is sufficiently rare to rank as a great Natural Wonder. We are told on good authority that these basaltic columns own their origin to tremendous lava upheavals breaking through the earth's crust to cool as the fantastic shapes we see here. Most of the columns are hexagonal, though a variety of other arrangements of from three to nine sides are also to be found.

The geologists have a strong case, but when it comes to holding an audience they are a poor match for the weaver of legendary tales who knows full well that the real builder of this architectural extravaganza was none other than Fionn MacCoul, a local giant who in ancient times laid out the causeway so that a contemporary Scottish giant would have no excuse against coming over to meet him in battle. But if neither of these explanations wholly convinces, consider instead the theory advanced by an over-learned nineteenth-century writer who claimed that the columns were the petrified remains of giant bamboos.

THE CITY HALL, BELFAST

In 1896 the old White Linen Hall which stood on this site was pulled down to make way for the proposed opulent new City Hall. The selected design was submitted by Alfred Brumwell Thomas of London, architect of several notable municipal buildings in England. The Portland stone, Renaissance-style City Hall has a frontage of 300 feet and stands 173 feet high at the top of the central dome. The interior makes considerable use of marble, but the effect, when judged alongside the tastes of the early 1900s, is by no means excessively showy. At the front entrance, and just visible at the extreme left of the picture, is the regally imposing statue of Queen Victoria by Thomas Brock, unveiled by Edward VII in July 1903 (the building itself was not completed until 1906). Brock was also responsible for the Titanic memorial and the Harland statue (of shipbuilding renown) in the grounds.

This worthy building is the hub of city life with all the main thoroughfares converging at this point; and the interior too is well known to the citizens of Belfast since it houses administrative offices dealing with public matters, as well as the Council Chamber and Lord Mayor's Parlour. But despite the hustle and bustle as Belfast goes about its business and the sounds of traffic never far away, it is still possible to enjoy lunchtime band concerts on its green lawns in summer and glimpse familiar hills between long avenues of tall buildings.